To get your free printable of these scriptures (in color) of the full size go to:

www.craftwithchristie.com

Find me on Social Media under

Create with Christie

on Facebook, Instagram, Pinterest and Youtube

A HandLettering and doodle Workbook

© Christie Daugherty. All rights reserved. No part of this publication may be reproduced, distributed, or transmitted, in any form or by any means, including photocopying, recording, or other electronic device or mechanical methods, without prior permission of the publisher, except in the case of brief quotations embodied in critical reviews and certain other noncommercial uses permitted by

Howdy Ya'll! That's a fancy greeting from my home state, Texas. :)

Thanks so much for purchasing this workbook. I'd love to take a minute and thank God for giving me the desire and passion for creativity and connecting women. Ya'll have blessed me so much. I'm so grateful!

This workbook is made up of 4 sections:

1. Drills & Practice

Practice, practice, practice! That is essential for improving your hand-lettering skills. You can put tracing paper on top of the pages so you can practice the same pages over and over.

2. Doodles

I've included steps on how to draw a simple banner and flower. Hopefully this will give you direction on how to break down steps for all the doodles I've included in the workbook. Feel free to trace them as well. The more you practice, the better you'll get!

3. Traceables

Tracing helps you learn different strokes and ideas of layout. Feel free to trace my designs for your own use. You could even frame them and give them as gifts.

4. Hand-Lettering Plus

The last section of the book is a sample intended to inspire you to take your hand-lettering to the next level. Although, It's fun to just write pretty, there's SO MANY things you can do with it when you add watercolor, inks, chalk markers and more! Maybe there will be a "Handlettering Plus" book if I find there is interest?

I'd love to invite you to share feedback on the book and anything I post on social media. Please reach out, I love meeting my followers so don't be shy! Anytime you post something inspired by or from the book I'd love if you'd use the hashtag #letterwithchristie.

Blessing and love,

Christie

Supplies...that is the question

Many of you want to know what supplies to use. Well, that really is different for everyone. And you'll want to use different supplies for different projects. After researching other Handlettering artists, there are a few common favorites as of when this book was published.

1. A Pencil

Some people prefer mechanical pencils and others a regular pencil. Just keep in mind you'll want to use it very lightly. The goal is to erase your strokes after copying over them in pen.

2. Tombow Dual Brush Markers

They are great for multiple purposes. I love that you can blend them and get an ombre effect and watercolor with them. It's also nice to have dual brushes of the same color.

3. Fudenosuke Brush Pen, Soft Tip, Black

This is also made by Tombow. I love this pen for smaller projects such as addressing envelopes, making my scripture cards and writing letters.

4. Uni-Ball Signo Broad Point Gel Pen

This is by far the best white gel pen I've ever owned. Some people complain about it skipping ink. My suggestion would be to write slow and steady. Hold you pen up so the ink flows down. It works wonderful on dark or Kraft paper. I also use it to make highlights on my brush lettering.

5. **Marker paper:** Rhodia Pad, Canson XL Marker or Bristol, Stathmore Bristol

6. **Tracing paper:** Strathmore, Use tracing paper throughout the book if you don't want to write in your book or if you want to use it for another project.

The above are my must haves at this moment but I'm alway open to trying new pens to add to my collection. I'd love to hear your feedback on your favorite markers.

7. Crayola Marker

Perfect for practicing! Use the broad side to get thick downstrokes.

So, now that you have an idea of what supplies hand letterers love, let's get started.

Drills and PRACTICE

Practice Makes Better

Basic Strokes
trace and practice →

all downstrokes are **THICK** *and all upstrokes are* THIN

Upstroke — light pressure

downstroke — normal to heavy pressure

alternate up and down

overturn

underturn

oval

loop

triple loop

descending stem loop

Brush Lettering

start here aaa aaa

start BBB BBB

start CCC CCC

start DDD DDD

start EEE EEE

start FFF FFF

start GGG GGG

start HHH HHH

III III

Lower Case

a a a a a a
b b b b b b
c c c c c c
d d d d d d
e e e e e e
f f f f f f
g g g g g g
h h h h h h
i i i i i i

j j j j j j

k k k k k k

l l l l l l l l

m m m m m m

n n n n

o o o o o o o o

p p p p p p

q q q q q q

r r r r r r

s s s s s s s

t t t t t t

u u u u u

v v v v

w w w w

x x x x x x

y y y y y y

z z z z z z

Faux-ligraphy

faux = FAKE

instead of using a brush pen, you can fake it to achieve the same look when making all your downstrokes thick.

TRY IT:

1	2	3
write words	downstroke LINES	color in
love	love	love
happy	happy	happy
smile		
fun		
joy		

your try

practice your FAUX

↙ DOWNSTROKE
✓ this NOT ~~this~~

it's ok to be fake

✓ **this** NOT ~~**this**~~

your turn ↘

cute as a button
sweet as a peach
bless your heart
over yonder
worn slap out
hold your horses
well, I declare
heavens to betsy
can't never could
hush your mouth

good job!

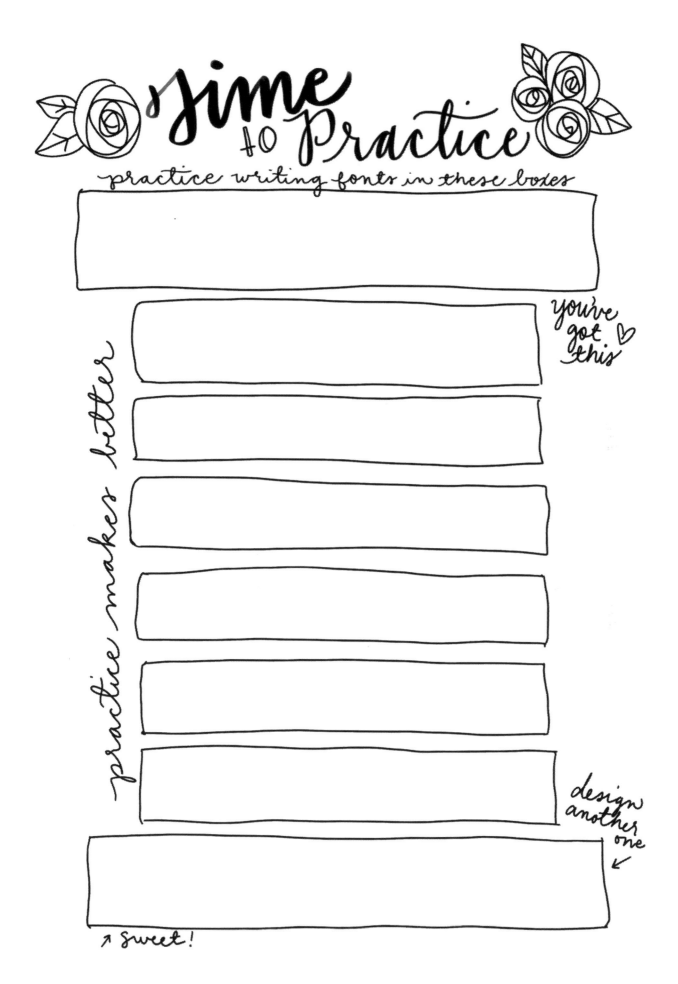

Letter Variations

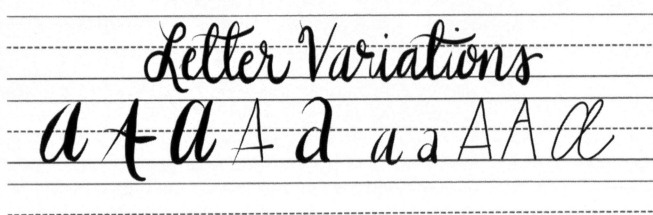

Ff Ff FF Ff Ff Ff ff

Gg gg Gg gg Gg GG Gg

Hh Hh hh HH Hh Hh H

Ii Ii II Jj Ii Ii Ii

Jj jj Jj Jj jj JJ Jj

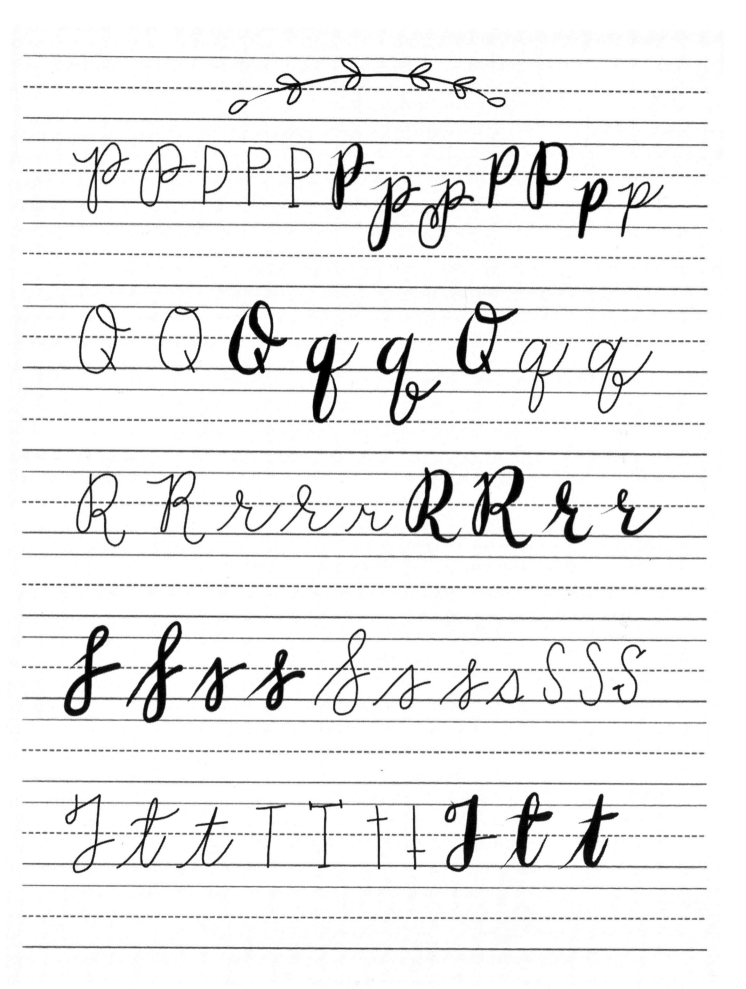

Z Z z Z z Z Z z

numbers

1 one 1 · 2 2 two · 3 3 three

4 4 four · 5 five 5 5 · 6 six 6

7 7 seven · 8 eight 8 · 9 nine 9

Bounce Lettering

Reg: happy

bounce: happy

ASCENDER LINE

x-height

DESCENDER LINE

(SAMPLES)
forever
wedding
bridesmaid
whatever
shower
bounce
pretty

go above and beyond the ascender and descender lines. Letters bounce up and down. The challenge is to make the words look balanced. It takes experimenting and practice.

princess

princess

Bounce Practice

happy   happy

hope   hope

blessed   blessed

easy   easy

today   today

plus   plus

kisses   kisses

patience   patience

apple   apple

sun shadow

Imagine you have a light source that shines on your word. You'll make contrasting lines where the shadows should be.

You TRY

1. pen line — *love* →
2. dot — **love** →
3. marker line — **love** →
4. double shadow — **love** →

↑ Try using a marker + pen.

---

add a shadow to these words. Try different styles.

Highlighting

Use a white gel pen to make accents or highlights. You can accent curves, downstrokes, make patterns, or whatever strikes your fancy!

I like using Signo uniball white and metallic gel pens.

curves → **love** →

pattern → **hope** →

dots → **peace** →

lines → **kind** →

right side → **faith** ~~→

happy →

varying sized dots → **smile** →

{ Did you notice the shadows too? }

♡ you try! ♡

Layouts and COMPOSITION

- arrangement into specific proportion
- the way text or images are arranged

let's try it

1. Choose a quote, saying, etc...

   Ex: YOU ARE INVITED to PAISLEYS' PARTY.

2. Sketch (or trace) a shape in pencil.

   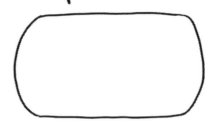

3. Write your key words larger.

   INVITED *Paisley's*

4. Fill in other words. Use different fonts and different sized pens.

   YOU ARE INVITED to *Paisley's* PARTY

5. Erase the shape.

   YOU ARE INVITED to *Paisley's* PARTY

6. Now you can polish it up, trace with markers and erase pencil lines.

   YOU ARE INVITED to *Paisley's* PARTY

★ now you try it on the next page →

↓ your turn

↘ try it!

hello HAPPY THANKSGIVING
thanks Happy Easter
bless you HAPPY VALENTINE'S DAY!
I'm sorry Happy Anniversary
miss you
Merry Christmas HAPPY New Year
Happy Easter I love You ♥
Bon Voyage
We've Moved! With Sympathy
Surprise new baby
HAPPY father's / mother's DAY!

→ Practice writing greetings

Congratulations
Congratulations
congratulations
Congratulations
CONGRATULATIONS
Congrats Congrats
Best Wishes
You Did It! Awesome Job!
hip hip hooray!

Connecting Letters

Trace the connecting letters ↓

a a - app act also sat

b b - blue able bat barber

c c - capable accept act

d d - da de add idle odd

e e - each egg beg segway

f f - after friend fun if

g g g - great ag gh ago

h h h - happy oh with hi

Dot your i's.

i i - is sick icicle

Can you spell it? ↓

Mississippi Mississippi

j j - jam jeep jump
k k - keep kite ok
l l - lamp old
m m - man am om
n n - no on
o o o - on over so
p p p - ap open
q q - quick squak
r r - risk or
s s - is so os
t t - to other

notice how letters may connect in different places

u u - **ugly bun**

v v - **over venture**

w w - **we cow**

x x - **x-ray ex ox**

y y - **yes dry**

z z - **zebra ooze**

Always be thinking about the next letter so you know where to end the last stroke.

Doodles

to scribble absentmindedly

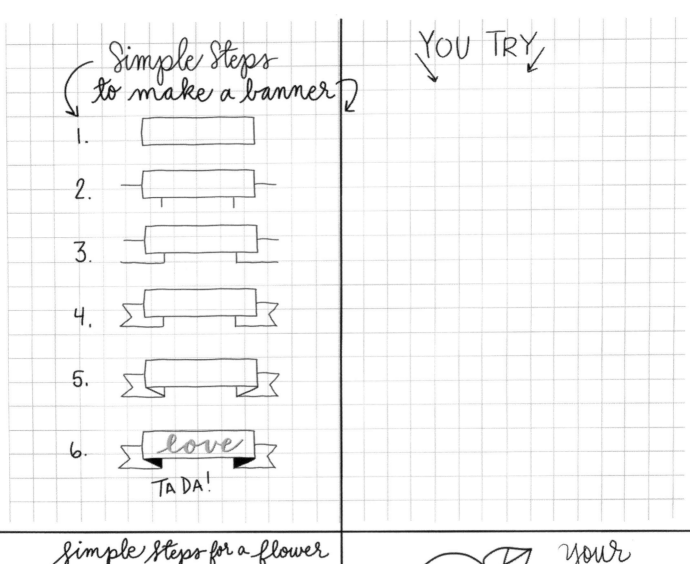

YOU TRY

Simple steps to make a banner

1.
2.
3.
4.
5.
6. love

TA DA!

your turn

simple steps for a flower

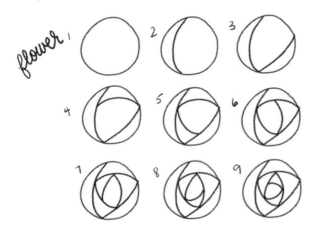

flower 1 2 3
4 5 6
7 8 9

leaves 1 2 3 4

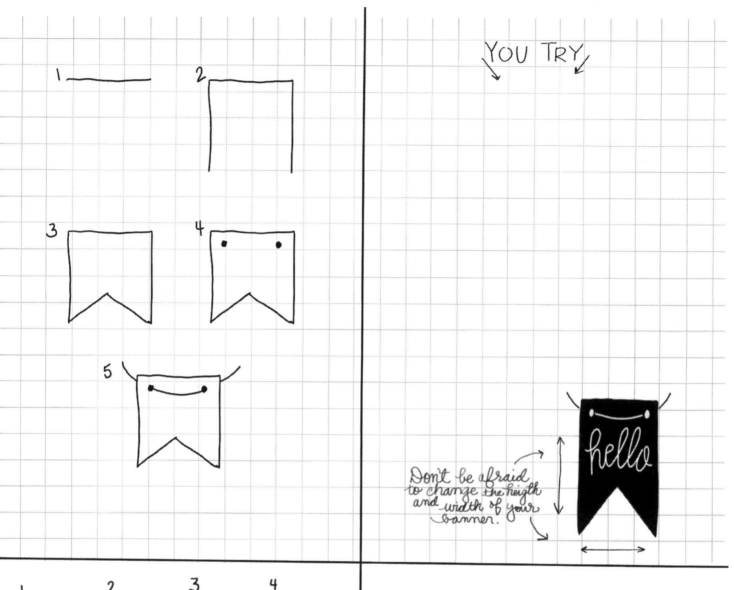
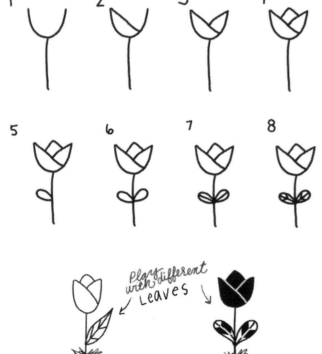

Doodles: florals

Practice your flowers

long stems?
short stems?
round petals?
pointed petals?

what are your favorite flowers?

Be inspired by nature around you → *colors, shapes + textures*

Doodles: arrows
and teepees

PRACTICE *tee pees AND arrows*

Doodles: trees

PRACTICE drawing trees

practice PLANTS
· copy or design your own ·

try a wilting plant

sketch a plant from real life

Decide if your leaves will be big or small

Draw a variety of POT styles

Doodles : Lines

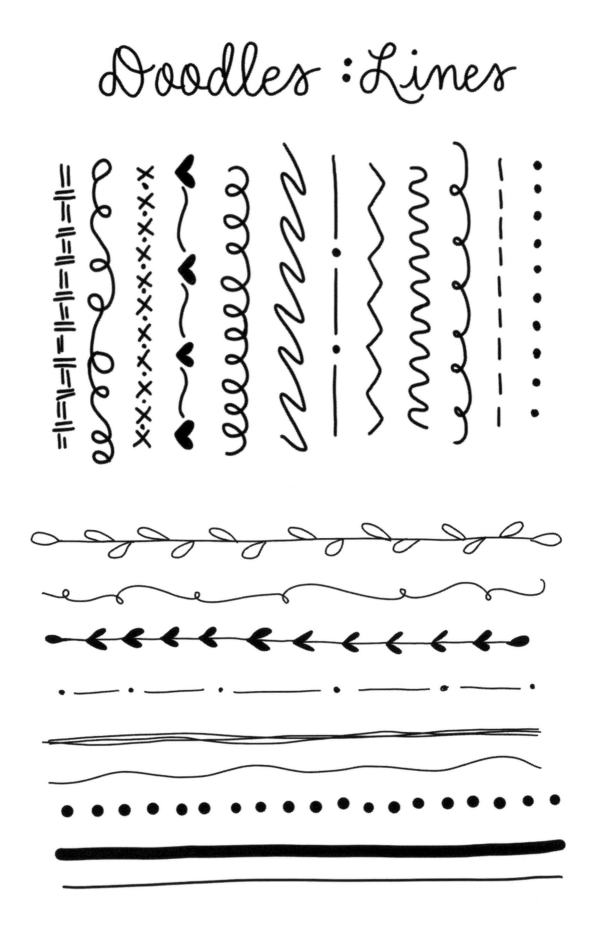

Doodles: Feathers

Practice drawing feathers

practice drawing flourishes

Practice banners

trace

to copy by drawing over its lines

Suggestion: use tracing paper
(for personal use only)

Let us hold unswervingly to the hope we profess, for He who promised is faithful.

Hebrews 10:23

© copyright Christie Daugherty 2013

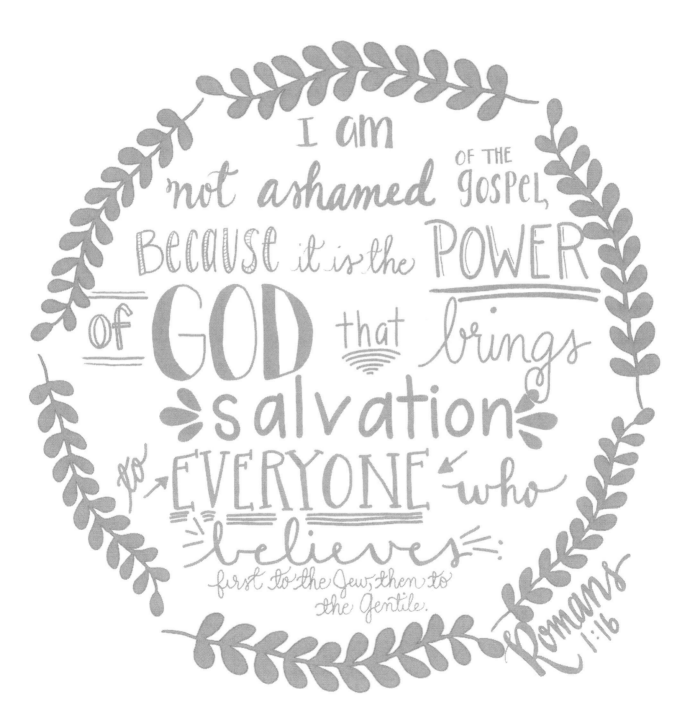

Let the message of Christ dwell among you richly as you teach and admonish one another with all wisdom through psalms, hymns, and songs, from the Spirit singing to God with gratitude in our hearts.

Colossions 3:16

© copyright Christie Daugherty 2018

"For I know the plans I have for you," declares the Lord, "plans to prosper you and not to harm you, plans to give you hope and a future.

Jeremiah 29:11

the joy of the Lord is my Strength

Nehemiah 8:10

For all have **SINNED** and fall short of the **GLORY** of **God.** and are justified by **HIS** grace as a gift, through the redemption that is in **CHRIST JESUS.**

Romans 3:23-24

— Romans 8:28 —

and we know that those who love **GOD** — all things work together for **good** for those who are called according to His **PURPOSE**.

"There is no condemnation for those who are in Christ Jesus. For the law of the Spirit of life has set you free in Christ Jesus from the law of sin and death."

— Romans 8:1-2 —

© copyright Christie Dougherty 2018

For the wages of sin is death, but the FREE GIFT of God is eternal life in Christ Jesus our Lord.

—Romans 6:23—

© copyright Christie Daugherty 2018

copyright © Nicole Daugherty 2017

Free journaling freebies - Nativity

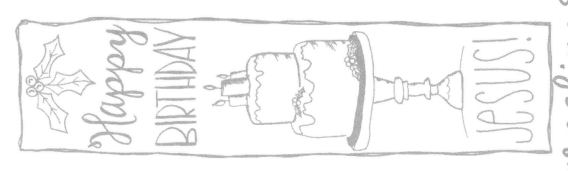

Bible Journaling Templates for margins.

www.sweetpeopineful.com

♡ Design your own inspiration cards ♡

Hand-Lettering Plus

Now that you've gone through this workbook, are you inspired to continue Hand-lettering? If so, you might be interested in my 6 week online course or joining my membership group. You can find out more by visiting and subscribing to my website.
www.craftwithchristie.com

What else can you do with hand-lettering and doodling?

- Card making
- Bible journaling
- Canvas art
- Chalkboard art
- Framed art
- Signs
- Scrapbooking
- Writing letters
- Addressing envelopes
- Any educator who does displays
- Any profession where you write on a board
- And more!

What kinds of techniques or mediums can you use with hand-lettering and doodling?

- Watercolors
- Inks
- Chalks
- Painting
- Ombre effects
- Heat embossing
- And more!

If you'd like to see some examples of these techniques, follow me on facebook and instagram at **Create with Christie.**

If you are interested in shopping my Scripture line of gifts and downloads, you find them on my website.

NOTICE: My website is CRAFT with Christie, not to be confused with my business name, Create with Christie. Unfortunately, the domain name Create with Christie was already taken.

Create With Christie

You can find several scripture downloads in my online store.

I teach online and in person craft classes. ♥

Look! It's me teaching an online class!

Don't forget to get your free PRINTABLE (IN COLOR) on my website!

Should I offer a class?

IPAD ART — I love designing and playing with my IPAD pro and Apple Pencil.

Hi, I'm Christie and I love what I do. I'm from East Texas where it's hot and humid, the people are friendly and you'll find a church and Mexican restaurant on every corner. I've been married to my husband, Duwine, since 1994. We have 2 amazing kids.

www.craftwithchristie.com

Punch Needle is a fun fiber art craft that is easy to learn. Watch a class preview on my website.

PUNCH needle

Have you ever heard of Bible Journaling? I ♥ it!

I hope to offer classes soon.

Bible Journaling

SWEET PEA PAISLEY
handmade gifts

find unique gift items on my website.

Sweet Pea Paisley is my handmade gift product line. I handletter scriptures and sew them onto gift items. My business name is special. My daughter's name is Paisley and my Dad calls her Sweet Pea ♥

www.craftwithchristie.com

Lord,

{ I pray for each person that goes through this workbook. My prayer is they will use their new hand lettering skills to bless others. Thank you God for your love, peace and understanding. We glorify you and know we can do nothing without you. }

If there is anyone reading this who hasn't accepted you as their Lord and Savior, I pray they will seek and find you.
John 3:16

You are an AWESOME God!

Amen,
Christie